Original title:
Searching for Meaning in the Middle of a Sandwich

Copyright © 2025 Creative Arts Management OÜ
All rights reserved.

Author: Elliot Harrison
ISBN HARDBACK: 978-1-80566-102-3
ISBN PAPERBACK: 978-1-80566-397-3

Beyond the Basic Bite

In a loaf of dreams, I take a seat,
With pickles dancing on my feet.
Lettuce whispers secrets, crisp and bright,
While mustard's laughter tickles the night.

Tomatoes ponder where they belong,
As bread insists they're all just wrong.
A sandwich tale with layers to peel,
Unraveled truths in every meal.

Waters of the Wrap

In a wrap, I sail through flavors vast,
Quick bites of joy, but none can last.
Spinach leaves, they wave hello,
While hummus currents start to flow.

Avocado dreams on a breezy shore,
With every munch, I long for more.
Yet in each fold, a giggle hides,
As I navigate these tasty tides.

Ephemeral Delights

A toast to bread as fluffy as clouds,
With toppings bold, it draws in crowds.
Cheese that melts like moments shared,
In this feast of fun, no one's scared.

Fries on the side act like they own,
While ketchup teases in a playful tone.
Between each bite, a chuckle flows,
As time slips by, like the last of prose.

Craving Something Deeper

Beneath the crust, a world so bright,
With every crunch, it feels so right.
A pickle's giggle, a bun's sweet smile,
This merry meal will last a while.

Yet there's a quest beneath the spread,
For flavors dancing in my head.
In each layer, a jester chimes,
Provoking laughter, tasting rhymes.

Whispers of Lunch

In the fridge, secrets dwell,
Between a pickle and a shell.
Lettuce whispers, sharing thoughts,
While bread contemplates its knots.

Tomato giggles, juicy bright,
As mayo dances, pure delight.
Each layer tells a tale anew,
Sourdough sighs, feeling blue.

Questions Between Bites

Why is the bread so soft today?
Is the cheese on a holiday?
Do the veggies feel the crunch,
As I savor this fine lunch?

Is the ham plotting a escape?
What's the sauce in this odd shape?
With every bite, I ponder deep,
As crumbs fall, secrets to keep.

Beneath the Mustard and Mayo

Under layers, dreams reside,
Mustard colors with pride.
Pickles hide and play their role,
As bread cradles the whole goal.

Lettuce flips, a crisp facade,
Tomato blushes, not a fraud.
Each spread holds a mystic cheer,
In this feast, all doubts disappear.

The Journey of Crumbs

Crumbs embark on wild exploits,
Falling down from tasty joys.
They traipse along the countertop,
In whimsical frolics, never stop.

Each sprinkle tells a funny tale,
Of flavors that never fail.
A crumb's adventure, small yet grand,
In my lunchbox, a wonderland.

Marinades of Memory

In a deli's embrace, dreams take a bite,
Condiments squabble, in the soft light.
Pickles dive deep, swimming for fun,
While lettuce shouts, "I'm second to none!"

Tomato slices debating their role,
Ketchup lurking, with goals on a roll.
Mustard's theory of layers unfolds,
As bread whispers secrets that never grow old.

The Sandwich Paradox

Two slices collide, a mystery swirls,
What lies in between? A universe twirls.
Are we the meat, or the bread's warm embrace?
In the realm of lunch, we ponder our place.

With every big bite, questions get loud,
Is this lunch for one, or a feast for a crowd?
The crumbs of our thoughts scatter on the plate,
A layering of flavors we slowly create.

Chewing Over Life's Questions

In the crunch of my crust, wisdom does hide,
As I munch on existence with pickle-filled pride.
Questions flow out like a mustardy stream,
"Is life just a sub, or more like a dream?"

I nibble on answers, each bite an insight,
The cheese melts away as I ponder the night.
Bologna rolls in, with a philosophical jest,
"Take a big bite, let laughter be your quest!"

Cheddar and Philosophy

In a world where the cheddar is sharp as a knife,
I ponder the sandwich that mirrors my life.
Is it stuffed with reflections or just plain old cheese?
Each layer unwrapped brings me moments like these.

A Swiss hole in the logic, a rye twist of fate,
With every good gulp, another thought waits.
Lettuce becomes wisdom, crisp, fresh, and bold,
As I snack on the stories that never grow old.

Sandwiches of the Soul

In the layers of bread, we ponder,
What lies beneath—lunch or wonder?
Lettuce whispers secrets, soft and green,
Tomatoes blush in the in-between.

Mayo dreams of being a star,
While pickles meditate, near and far.
Onions laugh with a tearful jest,
In this feast of thoughts, we find the best.

An Exploration in Every Bite

With each crunchy chomp, a new insight,
A deli delight in the morning light.
Mustard scribbles tales of yore,
While bread holds up a world to explore.

Cheese makes jokes that melt with glee,
As we munch on destiny, just you and me.
The crust concerns itself with fate,
Hoping we savor before it's too late.

The Meal Between Us

Between the layers, laughter brews,
Conversations seasoned with humorous views.
Jalapeños spice our debates,
While toasted buns hold our fates.

The platter smiles, a canvas so bright,
Whisking our worries away, light as a bite.
With each delicious squabble we share,
A sandwich saga unfolds in the air.

Spreading Thoughts Thin

Butter thoughts onto this wishful bread,
Spreading joy where worries are fed.
With a layer of jam, sweet and sly,
We toast to the dreams that refuse to die.

Peanut butter hugs the jam's brave taste,
In this quirky sandwich, there's no time to waste.
From crust to filling, our hopes entwined,
In the gooey goodness, our laughs are aligned.

Echoes Within the Ingredients

In the lettuce, whispers call,
Dreams of crunch and leafy brawl.
Tomatoes blush, thinking deep,
What secrets in this meal we keep?

Pickles giggle, let's not forget,
The mustard's tune, a tangy duet.
Bread's embrace, it holds us tight,
In this snack, the world feels bright.

The Sub's Secret

Beneath the layers, truth unfolds,
Salami tales and cheese that molds.
Can a hoagie truly know,
The paths of life where flavors go?

Jalapeños play the spice card right,
In a world that's savory and light.
But do they ponder, bite by bite,
Where did this journey start tonight?

Debates in Deli Meats

Ham insists it's the best pick,
While turkey rolls its eyes, quite thick.
"Salty or sweet?" the bologna sighs,
As melted cheese claims all the highs.

A pickle pipes up, all green and proud,
"Let's join together, make it loud!"
In this deli, decisions flow,
What's the best combo? Who will know?

Contradictions in a Coleslaw

In this bowl of crunchy fun,
Cabbage fights with dressing spun.
"Am I a side or main delight?"
Coleslaw laughs into the night.

Carrots argue in bright attire,
Who knew slaw could spark such fire?
With each forkful, laughter spills,
In this tub, nothing stands still.

The Philosophical Panini

In a crusty world, I ponder,
With cheese that melts and dreams that wander.
Lettuce wraps my hopes so tight,
As tomatoes shine, oh what a sight!

Between the slices, wisdom's found,
Mustard dreams, oh so profound.
A grilled debate on who we are,
With every bite, I raise the bar.

Taste Buds of Truth

Seasoned thoughts on toasted bread,
A dash of laughter, no fear or dread.
Pickles of pride, they crunch and sway,
In the condiment chaos, we laugh and play.

Ketchup drips like drops of fate,
With chips on the side, it's never too late.
Dip into joy, what flavors spark,
In every layer, we leave our mark.

The Yearning Between the Layers

Between the layers, whispers tease,
Intentions wrapped like melted cheese.
An avocado's touch, soft and bold,
Secrets and cravings both unfold.

Pressed to perfection, the quest ignites,
In the blend of flavors, our delight ignites.
Yet as I munch with blissful glee,
I ponder the meaning, could it be me?

Nourishment for the Soul

Beneath the crunch, a quest unfolds,
Craving a tale that never grows old.
With every bite, a giggle shared,
In this feast of fluff, no heart is spared.

Banana peels and a splash of zest,
In the realm of bites, we find our quest.
Let's savor the silly, the joy of the roll,
For life's a sandwich, we nourish the soul.

The Quest Beneath the Lettuce

In the land where pickles roam,
A journey starts from my lunch dome.
Two slices of bread, a bridge so wide,
Adventure waits where flavors hide.

A lettuce leaf, a mighty shield,
In mustard dreams, my fate is sealed.
I dig deep for treasures rare,
Finding crumbs? I do despair.

Oh, tomato, ripe and round,
Your juicy secrets not yet found.
Between each layer, I'm compelled,
To find the tales that none have yelled.

As I munch and chew with glee,
What is the meaning? Please tell me!
With each crunchy bite I crave,
Is it wisdom I hope to save?

Essence of the Everyday

Amidst the layers, I explore,
The essence trapped, can't take much more.
Between two slices lies my fate,
What's the deal with all this weight?

A slab of cheese, a creamy dream,
Could it reveal the grander scheme?
With each chomp, I ponder fate,
Is lunch-given thought worth the wait?

In every bite, a long-lost tale,
Residing in my lunch's veil.
Is there a truth beneath this ham?
Or simply cravings on the program?

So I laugh and take a taste,
Chasing thoughts, it feels like haste.
Could the answer be so sweet?
Or just the ketchup's sticky treat?

Between Bites of the Mundane

Crunchy edges, a world unfolds,
Each bite whispers of stories bold.
Lost in the layers, flavors collide,
In this embrace, my thoughts abide.

Is that a hint of yesterday?
Or just crumbs leading me astray?
With every nibble, the question grows,
What does life mean? Only bread knows.

Crispy bacon, oh, do you see,
The essence of deep philosophy?
In the mundane, I seek delight,
Juggling lunch in the midday light.

So, I munch in laughter's ring,
Is there wisdom in this fling?
One last bite, and then I'll know,
The secret hidden in my dough.

Savory Dreams and Lost Thoughts

In a world where crumbs collide,
Savory dreams try to abide.
Between the bites of things unspoken,
What did I think? The trance is broken.

Lettuce whispers, and cheese does laugh,
As I ponder the curious path.
Should I dissect this meal so grand?
Or just enjoy and take a stand?

A sandwich, bold, like tasty fate,
Each flavor tells a story, great!
But in this chaos, I confess,
What's the point? Oh my, I guess.

As mustard drips and mayo gleams,
I chase the truth in silly dreams.
With each hearty bite I take,
Is it laughter, or just my mistake?

Relishing Life's Compounds

Between two slices, wonders hide,
A pickle's grin, a mustard slide.
Tomato flirts with lettuce green,
In this feast, a joyful scene.

A sprinkle here, a dash of that,
Who knew lunch held such a chat?
Each bite reveals a tasty truth,
In every nibble lies our youth.

The Quest Beyond the Crunch

With chips on side and sauce to dip,
We embark on a flavor trip.
The crusty edges call us near,
What's lurking here? Oh, bring me cheer!

Like knights in aprons, brave we are,
Fighting crumbs, our lunch bazaar.
With every crunch, we shout hooray,
Adventure waits in bread's ballet!

Flourishing Between Flavors

Sliced bread hugs all the best delights,
Like friends who share our silly fights.
Piled high with tales no one can tell,
   A gooey center casts a spell.

With every bite, we laugh and sigh,
  As flavors dance and spirits fly.
  A curious mix, a layered play,
 In every sandwich, joy will stay.

Discoveries in Deli Dynamics

In the deli line, we face our fate,
As meats and cheeses congregate.
What's that in there? A secret swirl?
A bite of pickles! Let laughter unfurl.

A taste explosion, what a fumble!
Gherkins giggle, lettuce grumble.
Discoveries await in every stack,
With sandwiches, there's no looking back!

Crunching on Curiosity

Between two slices, ideas collide,
A pickle's wisdom, a tomato's pride.
What lurks in the lettuce, fresh and green?
A riddle of flavor, not yet seen.

In the mayo, a mystery spreads,
With whispers of garlic, it gently treads.
Do crumbs count as thoughts, or are they just waste?
As I chew on my questions, I savor the taste.

A Tasting of Truths

Layers of thought, like layers of bread,
What's toasted is crispy, what's soggy is dread.
Bite into laughter, the zest of the day,
As mustard-filled musings hold sway.

In the lunchbox of life, what's packed tight?
An egg salad's secret brings delight.
What's fruity and nutty may tickle the tongue,
A sandwich of wisdom, forever young.

Dilemmas on the Deli Plate

On a plate of choices, I'm stuck with my funk,
Should I grab the pastrami or go for the junk?
Each slice is a sentence, the bread is the tale,
Between bites and laughs, I ponder and ail.

Should I pair with a chip or a carrot stick?
A crunch in the chorus, a salty flick.
Life's just like lunch - a mix of delight,
With a dash of confusion, and cravings in sight.

The Deep-Dish Dilemma

In a deep dish of decision, I sway and I sway,
Sauce drips like secrets, their tangy display.
Should I add more cheese, or keep it quite light?
Each slice is a giggle, a daring bite.

With layers like life, both sweet and bizarre,
I question my choices, near and far.
The crust holds my hopes, the filling my dreams,
As laughter erupts, or so it seems.

A Layered Philosophy

In a lunchbox lies a riddle,
In mustard's twist, a tale so middle.
Is it the mayo or the cheese that sings?
Or just the dance of all these things?

Lettuce whispers secrets crisp and green,
Between the bread, where have you been?
Pickles promise to reveal the zest,
But where's the meaning in this quest?

The Crunch of Realization

Bite down hard, what do I feel?
A crunch that claims, "Life's a meal!"
Ketchup splatters, a messy fate,
Between my thoughts, I contemplate.

Is the answer on the plate or in my mind?
In every crunch, there's truth to find.
A chip of insight, a slice of fate,
A sandwich served; oh, isn't it great?

Finding Wholeness in Halves

Two halves make a whole, they say it right,
But does the crust just hide the light?
A tomato's heart, sliced learnèd truths,
Wrapped in bread, unveiled like youths.

The essence dwells in bites we take,
In every flavor, we set to wake.
Dill on the side with dreams to chase,
In each torn piece, we find our place.

A Chew of Reflection

With each chew, I ponder life,
The cheese, the bread, the subtle strife.
Can a toast break the silence loud?
Or does it hide beneath the crowd?

Crispy edges of my thoughts do blur,
As lettuce jokes and doubts confer.
In bites so bold, I toss my fears,
This sandwich is all my hopes and cheers.

Relish the Journey

In a world of bread and cheese,
I ponder life with every squeeze.
Lettuce whispers tales untold,
While mustard dreams of days of old.

Pickles dance with glee and flair,
Tomato slices show they care.
Each bite a riddle, sweet or sour,
Unraveling life's secret power.

With every crunch, a thought appears,
What's life without some tasty fears?
A sandwich stacked to touch the sky,
Silly dreams make laughter fly.

So lift your crust, embrace the fun,
And relish journeys, every pun.
Between the layers, joy we find,
In a world that's quite unrefined.

Metaphors in Mayonnaise

Slathered thick, the truth resides,
In creamy chaos, wisdom hides.
Each glob a metaphor in paste,
For thoughts we ponder, dreams we chase.

A spread of hopes, a dollop of glee,
In every sandwich, who are we?
Lettuce cradles stories bright,
While mayo glistens in the light.

With every bite, embark anew,
On journeys vast, like flavors brew.
Silly thoughts on toast collide,
In mayonnaise, our whims abide.

So take a fork, or just your hands,
Life's messy mix is what it stands.
In jars and layers, we explore,
The scrumptious tales we can't ignore.

Addressing the Core

Within the crust, the heart beats loud,
Where crusty layers form a crowd.
The core is close, yet hard to reach,
Like hidden lessons life can teach.

Avocado stands firm, so green,
In every slice, a sense of scene.
An onion's tear brings laughter near,
As flavors blend, dispelling fear.

The middle ground can be quite sweet,
With every crunch, we find our beat.
So stack it high, let worries flee,
In every bite, discover me.

So toast to life, and all its fuss,
With peanut butter, jelly, and us.
At the core of every meal's delight,
Is humor, love, and sheer delight.

The Underbelly of the Bun

Beneath the layers, secrets murmur,
A soggy slice, where hopes can flummer.
Ketchup spills provide the thrill,
As every bite asserts the will.

We dig beneath the toasty sheen,
To find the wit that lies unseen.
A crusty joke, a laugh we share,
In every nibble, moments rare.

So flip the bun, let's take a glance,
At what lies deep within this trance.
With every laugh, a crumb to chase,
In sandwich tales, we find our place.

So grab a bite, let giggles run,
In the underbelly, life's just fun.
Together here, let's take a stand,
In a world of bread, let's make our brand.

Between Bread and Thoughts

Between the bread, I pause and chew,
Thoughts get lost in mayo glue.
Pickles dance in my mind's space,
I laugh at the crunch, a silly place.

The mustard smiles, a sunny hue,
As I ponder life with each savory view.
Tomatoes squish, a juicy debate,
A sandwich of life, oh, isn't it great?

Crusts of wisdom, toasted and warm,
Embracing flavors, a quirky norm.
In every bite, a question bites back,
What's the meaning of this flavorful snack?

With laughter and crumbs all around,
I discover joy where nosh is found.
Between bread and thoughts, I munch and muse,
In this deli of dreams, there's no time to lose.

A Crust of Contemplation

In the crust, I find a thought,
Between each layer, wisdom caught.
Why's my sandwich talking to me?
It's bread, not a therapist, can't you see?

Bologna laughs, the cheese takes flight,
As I ponder my plight, day and night.
Is it the lettuce that holds the key?
Or just a joke that's hard to foresee?

The sesame seeds sprinkle ideas wide,
On this hoagie of life, I take a ride.
Between bites, I muse on all I lack,
Yet still, there's joy in this cheesy snack.

So here I chew in crispy delight,
Finding answers, oh what a sight!
In crusty contemplation, I find my way,
The sandwich of thought savored every day.

Layers of Existence

In layers piled high, I seek my fate,
A tower of bread, perhaps it's fate.
With lettuce crisp, and thoughts so spry,
I question the universe as I munch and sigh.

Pickles whisper secrets, oh what a twist,
In this layered life, how could I resist?
The snack of existence, a taste of the real,
Every bite brings me closer to what I feel.

Dressing drips down like a sage's advice,
I ponder my purpose, and isn't it nice?
In this sandwich symphony, I find delight,
Combining all flavors, wrong feels so right.

So here I am, in this edible quest,
Finding meaning, while I digest.
With layers of existence, I take a chance,
In every crumby laugh, life's funny dance.

Unwrapped Mysteries

Unwrapped sandwiches, so full of cheer,
Inside each layer, mysteries near.
I bite into bread, what secrets reside?
Whispers of flavor that dance and glide.

Salami sings of a savory glee,
Tomato jokes, just for me.
As I unwrap life with each tasty bite,
I laugh at the questions, like a comedic light.

The herb blend prances, the mayo grins,
In this wrap of thoughts, where laughter begins.
I relish the crunch, the savory flair,
As puzzling meanings float through the air.

So grab a sandwich, let's dig right in,
In this spread of joy, let the giggles begin.
With unwrapped mysteries, I munch and play,
Finding humor in crumbs along the way.

Epiphanies on Toast

In the kitchen, crumbs fly high,
Spreading wisdom, oh my, oh my!
A toast to thoughts, warm and bright,
With buttered dreams, I take a bite.

Jelly swirls like destiny,
Peanut butter holds the key.
Slicing through the bread of time,
Each spread reveals a twist of rhyme.

A sprinkle of salt, a dash of glee,
Sandwich charts my mystery.
What lies within this hearty fare?
I chew on questions, if I dare.

In every layer, tales unfold,
Of mustard dreams and laughter bold.
So here I sit with croissant quest,
Finding joy in every jest.

Unfolding the Flavor of Life

Between the slices, wisdom waits,
Wrapped in lettuce, on my plate.
Tomatoes glisten, shining bright,
In each bite, there's sheer delight.

The mayo spreads like fate divine,
Capers dancing, oh so fine!
Crunchy pickles, tales they tell,
In this banquet, all is well.

Each layer stacked, a quirky tale,
Of cartwheeling ants and sea-salt whales.
Lettuce laughs, the cheese all grins,
As I indulge in life's sweet sins.

With every chew, the flavors clash,
Philosophy wrapped in a flash.
The sandwich speaks, oh what a gift,
In every meal, my spirits lift.

Layers of Reflection

I stack my thoughts like bread so fine,
A layer of laughs, a slice of time.
Mustard dreams and pickle fears,
Together mingle, bring the cheers.

The top is shiny, a sesame crown,
While secrets linger, upside down.
In between the layers deep,
Are laughs and wisdom that I keep.

Oh, the turkey tells a joke or two,
While cheese melts with a sunny view.
Avocado whispers soft and sweet,
In this banquet, life's a treat.

So take a bid, don't hold the knife,
Each sandwich speaks of love and strife.
I chew on moments, savor the play,
In each bite, I find my way.

Breadcrumbs in the Crust

In the crust, a treasure hides,
Forgotten crumbs of life's wild rides.
A sprinkle here, a dash of there,
Each flavor's hint, a quirky flare.

With every crunch, I laugh and sigh,
Finding joys that flutter by.
What's lost within the sandwich maze,
Turns into joy, sets hearts ablaze.

Relish dreams, and chips of cheer,
In this feast of tasty veneer.
Sandwich sculptures, life's a feast,
Finding fun in every yeast.

So nibble on those seasoned tales,
As each bite's laughter never fails.
With breadcrumbs trailing as I roam,
In every sandwich, I find home.

Dismantling the Delight

In layers thick, a hidden tale,
A pickle's grin, a mustard trail.
Tomatoes blush, lettuce shivers,
Mysteries lurk, in sauce it quivers.

Crunch and munch in a comical way,
Did I find wisdom, or just gourmet?
Each bite a journey, each crunch a cheer,
Exploring flavors, but where's the deer?

The Essence of Each Bite

Bread hugs tight, the filling's spree,
A dance of tastes, wild and free.
Pickles chuckle, cheese does snort,
In this meal, a sitcom's sort.

As I chew on dreams, I giggle and grin,
The quest for truth tucked under skin.
With every chomp, a riddle unfolds,
Are we just lunch? Or tales untold?

Ungrasping the Grains

A crusty edge, soft center found,
The search is on, on whimsy's ground.
Under layers of lunch, thoughts collide,
In each bite, a joyful ride.

Grains slip and slide, a laughter spree,
What's next, a voyage or a fancy tea?
Amidst the mayo, a giggling snack,
Life's little puzzles, on this joyful track.

The Sandwich as a Metaphor

Two slices meet, a union grand,
Inside, chaos, oh isn't it planned?
A slice of life, or just a joke,
Beneath the layers, my thoughts awoke.

In every munch, I ponder and pry,
Is the sandwich wise, or just a fry?
With each savory layer, I chuckle and muse,
A canvas of crumbs, where nonsense is fused.

The Void Between the Slices

In the land of crusts and crumbs,
Where pickles dance and mustard drums,
I wonder what's beneath the bread,
A treasure map, or crumbs instead?

A lettuce leaf, a rogue in flight,
Hiding secrets, oh, what a sight!
Tomato whispers, 'Can you hear?'
Or is that just a sandwich smear?

The mayo spreads its creamy lore,
While thoughts get lost forevermore,
In this deli of delights, I muse,
On all the strange paths I could choose.

Beneath the weight of layers thick,
The deeper truths come fast and quick,
Of roast beef dreams and cheese so bold,
An epic tale yet to be told.

Flavors of Existence

In a bun of life, we pile it high,
With onions sweet and a dash of sighs,
A sprinkle of joy, a dollop of fear,
Each bite a riddle, loud and clear.

Ketchup drips like thoughts at noon,
While mustard's tang hums a silly tune,
Between every crunch, the meaning bends,
As toasted edges start to blend.

A sprinkle of salt, a dash of hope,
In this layered world, I start to cope,
Each flavor tells a funny tale,
Of laughter shared on a sandwich trail.

So here I sit with crumbs on my face,
In this culinary, quirky space,
With lettuce leaves of wisdom bold,
Sandwich stories ready to be told.

Unraveling the Heart of the Hoagie

With a hoagie stacked, life's big reveal,
Inside the bread, how do I feel?
Salami dreams and veggie woes,
In this sub, where laughter flows.

Pondering flavors, a curious chase,
Why does it tickle, this doughy embrace?
A bite of mystery, a taste of jest,
In layers of joy, I search for rest.

The cheese melts calm on a chaotic day,
While onions linger, come what may,
Each ingredient wrapped in a dance,
This hoagie's got the best of chance.

So I unwrap this sandwich wide,
With flavors swirling right inside,
Who knew such depth could be so funny?
In hoagie heart, I find my honey.

Cravings for Clarity

A sandwich stacked with dreams and cheer,
A crunch of clarity, bright and clear,
Between the slices, humor flies,
With every nibble, a new surprise.

Sourdough thoughts and rye regrets,
In this feast, we place our bets,
On what lies hidden, what to reveal,
As layers peal back, I start to feel.

Avocado wisdom on a toasted slice,
Spreading thoughts, oh so precise,
The vibrant taste of a crumb-filled quest,
In this sandwich search, I find my zest.

So here I munch with glee and grin,
In every bite, life's truths begin,
With bites of laughter in hand, I see,
The savory joy of a sandwich spree.

A Tapestry of Taste

Between the bread, I wonder loud,
What secrets lie beneath this crowd?
Pickles whisper, tomatoes shout,
   Is this what life's all about?

A slice of cheese, a dash of fun,
Will it satisfy, or come undone?
Lettuce, crisp and dreams anew,
Can one delight in mustard too?

With every bite, the mystery grows,
   Is it the mayo or the prose?
Each crunch reveals a tale or two,
A sandwich story, just for you!

So take a munch, embrace the mess,
In every layer, life's a press,
Between the slices, echoes play,
   As I devour the silly day!

Unearthing Hidden Crumbs

In the depths of my lunch, I dig and pry,
What lies beneath, what's the reason why?
A crumb, a seed, a squished-up dream,
In this loaf might be the cream.

On this quest for crumbs I stand,
Fighting rogue mayo, wasn't planned,
What stories hide in crust so brown?
A treasure map in a toasted gown!

The journey starts with butter's glide,
Directions lost, but spirits ride,
A sprinkle of joy, a dash of zest,
In this adventure, I'm truly blessed.

So peer inside your lunchbox deep,
Where oddities and flavors leap,
A whimsy wrapped, a quest's delight,
In every bite, the silly's bright!

The Conundrum of Condiments

Oh, ketchup rivers, mustard waves,
Do they guide me, or just misbehave?
Should I trust the ranch, so creamy and nice?
Or join the sangria, oh, a bold slice!

These sauces dance, a crazy ball,
Which one will catch me, which will fall?
Dijon dreams or sweet teriyaki,
Pickles win, it's not so wacky!

In this jar of flavors, I find my muse,
Each little scoop, a perfect bruise,
To spread or dip, the world at stake,
A culinary puzzle I must partake.

So swirl the dressings, let them play,
In lavish pools, let them sway,
For in this meal, we twist and spin,
Life's full of flavor, where to begin?

Queries Between Layers

Layers piled high, will they reveal,
The questions I have, the zest I feel?
Is the lettuce crisp, or just a ghost?
Do we toast our truths, or just boast?

Beneath each slice, a tale unfolds,
Of childhood lunches and snacks bold,
The inquiry starts with ham's soft sigh,
Is this sandwich worth the try?

As I peel back the onion's tear,
I question the pickles, do they care?
Are avocados wiser than they seem,
Or just a spread in my lunchbox dream?

So let's unwrap these bites of lore,
With every munch, I crave some more,
In this layered life, I take my stand,
With crumbs of wisdom on my hand!

Cravings for Clarity

In the fridge I find a slice,
A lonely cheese, oh so nice.
Mustard whispers, 'Take a chance!'
Lettuce giggles, 'Join the dance!'

Tomato winks, so round and red,
But what's the meaning of this spread?
Each flavor bold, yet so unsure,
Am I the sandwich or the cure?

A breaded boat, afloat with dreams,
Of crispy crunch and tasty themes.
The pickle's cheeky, clinks your glass,
While crumbs of thought begin to pass!

I ponder deep, as I take a bite,
Is this the world, or just a plight?
With every chew, I laugh a bit,
Maybe zest is where it's at?

So here I stand, with sauce on hand,
With tiny thoughts like grains of sand.
A quest of condiments, oh so grand,
What's the lesson? Perhaps: just snack!

The Essence of Every Layer

Layers piled, a colorful sight,
Brimming with joy, a pure delight.
These aren't just food, they're tales galore,
Crunching whispers as they explore!

A hidden wish between the bread,
Is there a spark in this spread?
With every slice, a secret squished,
What exists here, in this dish?

Lettuce craves the summer sun,
While mayo dreams of cake and fun.
Each bite, a riddle yet unsolved,
The taste of life, so sweet, evolved!

Does a sandwich hold the key,
To truths that set the mind all free?
It might just be the toast we crave,
In every crunch, a path we pave!

So relish every thickened spread,
For laughter lies where crumbs are shed.
In every munch, a truth unfurls,
Through simple bites, we change the worlds!

In the Heart of the Meal

Amidst the chaos of passing plates,
A bun demands it all, then waits.
Sauces drip like offbeat tunes,
Creating symphonies 'neath the moons!

What lives within this crispy shell?
A tale of hunger, I can tell.
Veggies chat with bread, so bright,
In this culinary gig, what's right?

Pickles dance on the tongue with cheer,
With every layer, truth draws near.
Are these more than just delights,
Or clues to love between the bites?

Slices stacked, like moments shared,
Each flavor bursting, nothing spared.
As I chomp through, I laugh and sigh,
In this feast, impressions fly!

So, let me dive into this meal,
What's real and what's just a deal?
A tasting plate of life's grand game,
What's the lesson? Joy—no shame!

The Delicacy of Discovery

In between the bun so fine,
Lies a journey, yours and mine.
Bite by bite, we peel away,
The layers of this delicious play!

Avocado dreams and bacon cheers,
Each flavor whispers, quelling fears.
Crunch and squish, it's all a thrill,
Do we savor or seek the fill?

With each condiment, wisdom spreads,
Life's a banquet, not just breads.
At this table, laughter swells,
What stories surf on our taste-bells?

Perhaps the mayo holds the truth,
In this salty mix, our youth.
So I dig deeper with each bite,
Unraveling layers, pure delight!

So raise a toast to every spread,
For in each sandwich, dreams are bred.
A playful quest on a lunch break,
Who knew enlightenment could taste like cake?

Cradled in the Bread

In a loaf of life, I bite today,
Lettuce whispers secrets, in a wacky display.
Tomato giggles as pickles twirl,
Between slices of joy, my thoughts unfurl.

Mayo smiles, a creamy delight,
While mustard grins, ready for a fight.
On this picnic table, I feast and ponder,
What's found in a crunch, makes me wander.

Bacon jokes about the crispy phase,
Saying, 'Is this wisdom, or just a craze?'
I laugh at the thought, can it be true?
Between bites of chaos, I think of you.

So here in my meal, I seek to find,
A sprinkle of laughter, a dash of mind.
Feeling full of crumbs, yet somehow slight,
In each munch of this riddle, I take flight.

The Harmony of the Half

Half a sandwich, a curious quest,
Contents spilling out, feeling blessed.
A slice of humor, a dollop of cheese,
I giggle and munch, my mind's at ease.

The crust sings loudly, the middle hums,
Together they dance, making all kinds of drums.
Pickles join in with a crunchy beat,
A rhythm of savory, oh what a treat!

With each little bite, absurdity grows,
As condiments clash in quite funny shows.
Is it bliss or confusion—who really knows?
In this layered mess, my spirit glows.

So I toast to the halves, so perfectly paired,
In the sandwich realm, where no one's scared.
Finding a giggle within each strange lump,
Life's quirky flavor, oh what a jump!

Heartbeats Between the Bread

A heart-shaped crust, love's tasty frame,
Between two edges, things can get lame.
Slice of bologna, creeping forth,
Can it unravel the laughter's worth?

The cheese, it melts, like my funny bone,
While lettuce taps out a melody known.
Each sandwich heartbeat, a giggle shared,
In the layers of life, we're all prepared.

A mustard masquerade, calls out to the rest,
Inviting sweet stories, to join in the fest.
Crumbs of wisdom, trail behind,
In every good nibble, sweet truths unwind.

So let's bite down, on this playful thrill,
With every chomp, let's savor the chill.
Between the carbs, the world fits tight,
In this oddity meal, joy takes flight.

The Salty Search

In a sea of bread, I dive for the salt,
Finding puzzle pieces, is it my fault?
The olives wave, with a savory cheer,
Do they hold the wisdom I'm craving here?

Crunch of the chips, sounds like a song,
What's a lunch bunch without a bit of throng?
I sprinkle the humor, let laughter align,
In a world full of taste, I'm feeling divine.

With a side of confusion, I munch and I sip,
Dancing with crumbs that could make my heart skip.
Every bite unravels, odd mysteries swell,
In this crazy banquet, I'm under a spell.

So here's to each sandwich, silly and grand,
Crafting bizarre tales, with each greasy hand.
In the crusty delight, I find my way through,
Life's a strange table, and I savor the stew.

Toasted Thoughts

In the crisp warmth of bread,
I ponder what crumbs I've fed.
Is the mustard my muse, or just spread?
Is this laughter or just a dread?

Pickles dance on the side,
They giggle and they glide.
Between bites, I cannot hide,
This sandwich is my cherished guide.

Lettuce whispers to me,
'What's the flavor of glee?'
Tomato's vibrant decree,
Says something's meant to be.

The grill marks tell my tale,
In each bite, there's never fail.
With every layer, I set sail,
In this bun, I'll never pale.

Whispers in the Wrap

Beneath tortilla's soft embrace,
A mystery I cannot place.
Is it guac that sets the pace?
Or salsa's spicy, wild grace?

Each crunch echoes through the night,
Veggies in a colorful flight.
'Tis not just hunger's appetite,
But joy wrapped up oh so tight.

Avocado dreams within,
Sour cream's a cheeky grin.
What lies hidden in this din?
A giggle that will always win.

Lettuce whispers secrets sweet,
In a dance of foam and heat.
Every layer, oh what a treat,
Life's wrapped up in each bite's beat.

Between the Bread of Life

In the layers, I reside,
Flavors mixing side by side.
A pinch of fun, a dash of pride,
In every bite, my joys abide.

The crust may seem a little tough,
But inside, there's playful stuff.
Diving deep, I can't get enough,
Each snack's a giggle, never gruff.

Barbecue drips, what a thrill,
Chasing dreams with each big meal.
Is this absurd? Or just a deal?
In every moment, I will heal.

Here's to bread in life's great race,
Finding jokes in every space.
With every slice, I embrace grace,
In laughter, I shall always place.

Sauces of Self

In a jar sits aspirations,
Ketchup dreams and revelations.
With each dip, my heart's relations,
This flavor dance defies foundations.

Mayonnaise smiles with creamy wit,
While vinegar adds a quirky split.
Is life a drizzle? Just a hit?
Or a plate where laughter's knit?

My identity's a bold spice,
Sriracha brings the finest slice.
Each taste a chance to roll the dice,
In every flavor, I'll think twice.

So here's to my savory quest,
A sandwich life, I'm truly blessed.
In sauces thick, I find the jest,
In life's great meal, I'll never rest.

Beyond the Deep-Fry

In the fryer's dance, secrets swirl,
Potatoes plunge, as flavors twirl.
Behind the crunch, a tale does simmer,
Who knew a chip could be such a winner?

Catch the scent, what do we behold?
A crispy mask, a heart of gold.
With each munch, we laugh and chime,
Was that a tang? Or just bad brine?

A sandwich speaks, but does it know?
Between the bites, the giggles flow.
Lettuce whispers, cheese gives a grin,
In this buffet, we're all kin.

So raise a fry, to questions unsaid,
Why's the ketchup always misunderstood?
The truth is deep-fried, let's take a chance,
With a side of laughter, join the dance.

Tasting the Unwritten

Between two slices, tales unfold,
A mystery spread, both hot and cold.
What's lost in layers of mustard and ham?
Perhaps a fortune, or just a jam?

We nibble dreams, as crumbs take flight,
Each bite a puzzle, hidden from sight.
The pickles giggle, the mayo sighs,
In the world of sandwiches, no one ever lies.

With every chomp, we're authors anew,
Creating stories, taste buds accrue.
A toast to the laughter, joy's true theme,
The hotdog's line, a punning dream.

So savor the slice, let flavors collide,
In this culinary ride, take joy in the side.
Between the bites, what wisdom we glean,
It's the joy of cuisine, that remains unseen.

The Mystery of the Melt

Under the grill, secrets convene,
Cheese drips slow, a gooey sheen.
The toast awaits, a vessel of cheer,
What warmth awaits, when friends draw near?

The bacon crackles, a symphony sweet,
As laughter blends in with every treat.
Tomato slices whisper tales slight,
Of summer days bathed in golden light.

A bite takes you to a dreamy realm,
Where flavors mingle and hopes overwhelm.
What's hidden here, in the stretchy cheese?
Mayhaps the answers are meant to tease.

So lift your sandwich, with joy and delight,
Each crumb a promise, of pure appetite.
With giggles and stories, let's take our flight,
To the land of the melt, where hearts ignite.

Cured Questions and Open Answers

In a deli's haze, mystery lingers,
Meat-tinged wisdom, held by fingers.
A pastrami tale, with no clear end,
What do we crave? A savory friend?

In the sandwich realm, questions persist,
Do pickles yearn for a citrus twist?
With every crunch, we ponder away,
Is tomorrow filled with more rye or play?

Haikus of lettuce in whispering tones,
From tomato's pulp, we craft our bones.
Lettuce laughs, while bread shows its might,
What do you seek, when taking a bite?

So here's to the unknown filled with glee,
As gourmet dreams spill forth with tea.
In layers of goodness, let's find our stake,
For in each sandwich, there's joy to make.

A Journey Between Ingredients

In a bread boat I row, quite absurd,
With lettuce waves and mustard birds.
Tomatoes dance to a pickle tune,
Under the watchful eye of a napkin moon.

I ask the cheese, what lies beneath?
It chuckles, "Life's a little sheaf!"
Lettuce whispers secret delight,
In this sandwich, we take flight.

Bite after bite, I ponder and chew,
What's the point of pastrami, who knew?
The crust tells tales, both spicy and sweet,
As I savor the layers, each flavor a treat.

My quest was grand, for wisdom divine,
Instead, I found crumbs and some fine wine.
In each layer, laughter and glee,
This bunsome journey has set me free!

Aromas of the Soul

The scent of pickles fills the air,
With every whiff, I'm without a care.
Mustard dreams and mayo schemes,
In this lunchbox maze, nothing's as it seems.

Sandwich shop, a wise sage indeed,
Ingredients talk, from sour to sweet.
The bread and jam gossip in glee,
Flavors collide, how joyful to be!

Each bite a riddle, a frolic in taste,
Ketchup debates with a rye paste.
With each crunch, a slice of zest,
In this culinary quest, I am blessed.

So let's laugh at life, with a side of fries,
For amidst these fillings, the humor lies.
Between the layers, I find my role,
In every sandwich, the aromas of my soul.

Pickles of Perception

Nestled snug in this crunchy embrace,
Pickles grin with a curious face.
They whisper secrets, oh what a spree,
In tangy green, they jive with glee.

With onions dancing a pungent waltz,
I reflect on my life and its many faults.
The mayo slides in, all creamy and sly,
A culinary jest, oh my, oh my!

Each condiment checks in for a chat,
As a slice of ham dons a floppy hat.
Let's simmer our thoughts in this saucy brew,
For bread is the canvas, and we paint anew.

As I munch on philosophy wrapped in a bun,
A laugh erupts, for life is too fun.
In the tangle of tastes, I finally see,
The pickle's perception sets my mind free!

The Fillings of Identity

In the layers of life, what's really inside?
A salsa of stories, where I confide.
Tomato truths and onion regrets,
In this tasty journey, nobody forgets.

Peanut butter dreams stick to my heart,
While jelly winks, playing its part.
Each filling is me, both savory and sweet,
Between these slices, I find my beat.

Salami shares a laugh, thick and bold,
While a shy avocado tells tales untold.
With every bite, a morsel of me,
In this delicious dilemma, I'm finally free.

So here's to the journey, all mixed and combined,
In the sandwiches of life, we're perfectly lined.
Each flavor a piece of my grand history,
Together we savor this tasty mystery!

Filling in the Gaps

In the depths of bread, I explore,
What's the mayo really for?
Is it a hint of dreams untold,
Or just a way to keep it bold?

Lettuce whispers secrets sweet,
While tomatoes dance, their juice a treat.
I ponder the pickles, tart and bright,
Are they the answers, or just for spite?

Under layers, I dig and delve,
Finding bits of truth, I hope to shelve.
Each bite a clue, or so it seems,
Life's recipes are saucy dreams!

With each hearty munch, I frown and chew,
What's the purpose? Not a clue!
Yet laughter bubbles, my heart does flip,
In this feast, I take a trip!

A Sandwich of Significance

Between two slices, tales reside,
With cheesy grins, they cannot hide.
A crusty truth, in every chew,
What's the meaning hiding in view?

Pickles prance, a zesty crew,
With each crunch, they shout, "Oh boo!"
Are they the clues or just for taste?
In this good meal, there's no time to waste!

I lift the bun, like a great big lid,
Finding wisdom, or just a kid.
With mustard dreams and ham so proud,
Each flavor's voice, it sings aloud!

From condiments, I seek the fate,
Between two layers, just can't wait.
Each bite's a riddle, fun and sly,
In this delight, the answers lie!

The Taste of Introspection

Bread's a haven, warm and kind,
But what's the filling they designed?
With every bite, I twist and turn,
In the gooey goodness, I yearn!

The peanut butter's thick and rich,
Makes me wonder, is it a hitch?
Jelly wobbles like my thoughts,
In this meal, wisdom's sought!

I chew on thoughts like crusty edges,
With every crunch, I pledge my pledges.
Should I dip it or take it plain?
In this chaos, it's all a game!

So slice it up, let's feast and laugh,
Every layer, a quirky path.
In this creation, joy runs rife,
Taste-bud musings, the sandwich life!

Hidden Spices of Life

In the layers, spices bloom,
Where does joy find room to loom?
A dash of laughter, pinch of zest,
In each bite, life puts to test!

There's cumin hiding, playing coy,
Garlic whispers, "Don't be shy!"
Savoury secrets, tucked away,
Flavorful thoughts in bright array!

With each crunch, I grin and munch,
Finding answers in the lunch.
What's the reason for this feast?
A playful game, a tasty beast!

Beneath the crust, I've found my cheer,
Each ingredient calm my fear.
In this whirling, tasty dance,
Life's a sandwich—take a chance!

The Quest Beneath the Surface

In a lunchbox realm where mayo flows,
I question the fate of my meat and prose.
Pickles whisper secrets, crisp and bright,
While mustard dreams dance in the afternoon light.

Beneath these layers, a riddle lies,
Why do we feast, yet still disguise?
With each bite I ponder, lost in delight,
A quest for the truth in every sight.

The wheatbread cradles my thoughts so grand,
As crumbs fall like stars from a distant hand.
The lettuce giggles, the cheese does tease,
In this puzzling feast, I'm hoping to please.

A sandwich savior, my rolling feast,
Bringing together the odd and the least.
In flavors and textures, I find a new spin,
The joy of discovery thickens the skin.

Filling the Void

A slice of bread with a gap so wide,
What's inside it, I wonder, can't hide.
Jelly or jam, or maybe a smear,
What fills this void? I'm drawing near.

The tomato wonders if life's a charade,
While lettuce whispers, 'Don't be afraid!'
Is it the crunch or the gooey delight,
That makes my lunch dance into the night?

Peanut butter slathers on thick as a plot,
While honeycomb dreams make my thoughts quite hot.
With every bite, I'm lost in a sea,
Of pickled reflections that savor me.

So what fills the void in this gourmet race?
A mix of odd flavors—a curious space.
A laugh, a giggle, all wrapped up tight,
In this bready embrace, I find my light.

Between Two Slices

Between two slices, a world unfolds,
Where adventure brews and laughter scolds.
A championship of taste, a duel divine,
As I dive into layers that twist and entwine.

Tomatoa's pep talks the lettuce along,
'Together we're fierce, together we're strong!'
Onions shed tears as they chop and they dice,
While my stomach grumbles, 'Let's roll the dice!'

A pickle parade in a mayo dip,
Navigating flavor on a wondrous trip.
Every crunch echoes in symphonic cheer,
As I venture deeper, the message is clear.

In this edible tale of whimsy and zest,
I find what I seek—the joy of the quest.
So between these two slices, I take my stand,
Finding laughter and love—It's all so grand!

The Flavor of Identity

In a wrap or a roll, my tale does unfold,
With fillings to treasure, both seasoned and bold.
I'm saucy like relish, with a snap in my bite,
Revealing my layers, I beam with delight.

Identity's flavor, a mix so divine,
With each crunchy echo, my true self does shine.
A journey through spices, so quirky and bright,
As your taste buds giggle in the warmth of the night.

The treasure's concealed in my culinary skin,
A dance of sensations, where do I begin?
Between grains and greens, the echoes arise,
Each bite an adventure, a tasty surprise.

So come take a leap, enter this world,
Where flavors collide and stories are swirled.
In every delicious, absurd bite,
The flavor of identity is pure delight.

The Enigma of Edibles

Between the bread, a quest unfolds,
Where mustard whispers, and mayo scolds.
Each layer stacked, a tale to tell,
Is it love or lunch? I can't quite tell.

Lettuce laughs and tomatoes sigh,
Pickles ponder, oh me, oh my!
In this deli dance, we wiggle and sway,
Hoping for wisdom in crumbs along the way.

Onions peel back layers of fate,
Crispy bacon sings, it's never too late.
Delightful chaos within this bread,
What secret truths lie hidden instead?

So here I sit, my food affair,
In every bite, a puzzle to bear.
Between cheese and dreams, my heart shall roam,
In this edible mystery, I'm far from home.

In Search of the Perfect Bite

A quest for crunch and savory bliss,
In this towering creation, I can't help but miss.
Between the slices, I dive and explore,
A flavor-filled journey, who could ask for more?

Will it be spicy, or sweet and neat?
With each munch and crunch, I take a seat.
The quest for the perfect, oh what a feat,
To discover joy at the edge of my treat!

As ketchup drips, I smirk at fate,
Each condiment whispers, it's never too late.
From crust to crust, my cravings ignite,
In this grand adventure, all feels just right.

So stack it high, and roll the dice,
For one perfect morsel, this must suffice.
In every sandwich, a mystery hides,
With laughter and crumbs, my appetite glides.

Seeking Substance in the Spread

A smear of cream and dollops of jam,
Each bite a riddle, oh, where's the slam?
With every layer, I gather and blend,
In this wonderful mess, where flavors extend.

Peanut butter dreams and jelly laughs,
Dive into this tangle of edible halves.
Where's the meat? Where's the cheese?
In this flavorful jungle, I'm begging, "Please!"

With every layer, I plot and I scheme,
Pondering the logic in this quirky dream.
A dance of deli delights, wooing my heart,
In each tasty swirl, is this just the start?

So assemble my feast, with joy I implore,
In layers of laughter, let's open the door.
For within this spread, the true treasures lie,
In crumbs of good humor, my thoughts freely fly.

The Heart of a Hero

Between the breads, a hero shall rise,
With pickles and ham, a feast in disguise.
Armed with a napkin and great appetite,
I venture forth, ready to fight!

Chasing that gusto with gusto I chase,
In this sandwich stalemate, I take my place.
The lettuce stands strong, the bacon's a knight,
Together they battle, ready for bite!

With each brave encounter, a crunch of delight,
In this epic saga, I savor the night.
Sauces may drizzle, but spirits won't fall,
For within this creation, I'll conquer it all!

So here I feast, bold hero am I,
In each playful layer, I reach for the sky.
To clasp my sandwich, like sword in the fray,
With laughter and joy, I devour the day.

Spices of Existence

In the fridge, a pickle winks,
Ketchup muse, my brain just blinks.
Mustard thoughts on toasted bread,
Life's a feast, or so I've said.

Lettuce whispers secrets green,
Tomato's blush, a sight unseen.
Onion layers bring a tear,
But grilled cheese brings me all the cheer!

A slice of ham, a turkey quest,
In every bite, I seek the best.
Juggling flavors, giggles reign,
A symphony of joy, no pain!

If life's a sandwich, pass the spread,
With every crunch, new thoughts are fed.
So let's devour, bite by bite,
This tasty dance from morning's light.

Exploring the Unseen Bite

Between the bread, adventures hide,
A fairground ride, a thrilling slide.
A chip of crunch, a splash of zest,
What's in here? A taste test quest!

Beneath the lettuce, dreams may lay,
In mustard shadows, lost play.
The mayo's grip, a slippery thrill,
What's life's purpose? Let's have a grill!

A bearded man in a submarine,
Bites of wisdom, ever unseen.
With every layer, flavors collide,
Finding laughter on this culinary ride.

So munch away, uncurl your mind,
In every crunch, what truths you'll find!
An exploration within each bite,
From the first taste to sheer delight!

Epiphanies in the Fillings

In bread's warm hug, ideas bloom,
Silly thoughts escape the gloom.
Every filling tells a tale,
In turkey's dance and ham's reveal.

With pickles marching, proud and tall,
Life's puzzles mix in the squall.
Bite into dreams, let flavors burst,
Amongst the crumbs, joy's rehearsed.

Avocado whispering, soft and green,
In every layer, laughter's sheen.
The Swiss cheese giggles, holes so grand,
In every nibble, we take a stand.

Unwrap the joy, toss doubts away,
Life's a sandwich, come what may.
With every layer, we grow bold,
In crispy bites, new stories told!

Saucy Contemplations

Tomato relish, what a perk,
In each splash, I find my quirk.
A drizzle here, a swirl of that,
Life's a dance, a playful spat.

Salsa dreams on tortilla wraps,
Wisdom hidden in crispy snaps.
Every condiment, a twist of fate,
As we ponder, "What's on my plate?"

Olive oil, a drizzle of thought,
In every sandwich, lessons caught.
With each bite, the world's unveiled,
Fun with flavors, thoughts regaled.

So pile it high, don't hold it back,
In this banquet, find your track.
With chopped veggies and meats galore,
Let's toast to life, forevermore!

www.ingramcontent.com/pod-product-compliance
Lightning Source LLC
Chambersburg PA
CBHW051657160426
43209CB00004B/928